Look and See

ACTIVITY BOOK

Gregg Schroeder

Back to School 2

Unit 1   In Class 4

Unit 2   Weather 10

Unit 3   My Community 16

Unit 4   Make Some Noise! 22

Unit 5   Shapes Around Us 28

Unit 6   Can You Swim? 34

Unit 7   At Home 40

Unit 8   My Special Place 46

Unit 9   Under the Sea 52

Unit 10 Picnic Time 58

NATIONAL
GEOGRAPHIC
LEARNING

Australia • Brazil • Mexico • Singapore • United Kingdom • United States

T0045456

Back to School

1 TR: 0.1 Listen and match. Then say.

1 2 3 4

1 TR: 0.2 Listen and chant. Then say.

Monday	Tuesday	Wednesday	Thursday
1	2	3	4

Friday	Saturday	Sunday
5	6	7

In Class

1 TR: 1.1 Listen. Circle ✔ or ✘.

1 (✔) ✘

2 ✔ ✘

3 ✔ ✘

4 ✔ ✘

5 ✔ ✘

6 ✔ ✘

7 ✔ ✘

2 Point and say.

NEW WORDS: *count to ten, draw a picture, make a craft, play a game, read a book, sing a song, write letters*

1 TR: 1.2 Listen and match. Then point and say.

1 2 3 4 5 6 7

1 TR: 1.3 Find and say. Then listen and sing.

2 Write ✔ or ✗.

VALUE   **Work hard at school.**

1 ☐

2 ☐

3 ☐

1 TR: 1.4 Listen and trace. Say.

2 Trace.

1

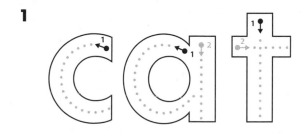

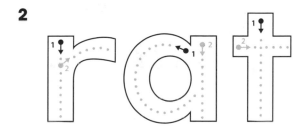

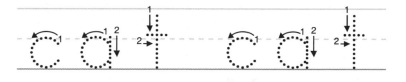

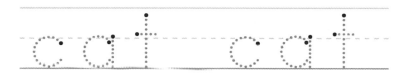

2

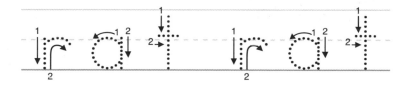

1 Match. Color and say.

$9 + 1 = 10$

$3 + 1 = 4$

$5 + 1 = 6$

VIDEO: SC: 2 (optional)   **Content Words:** *add, cupcake, more*

1 Say and color. Then play.

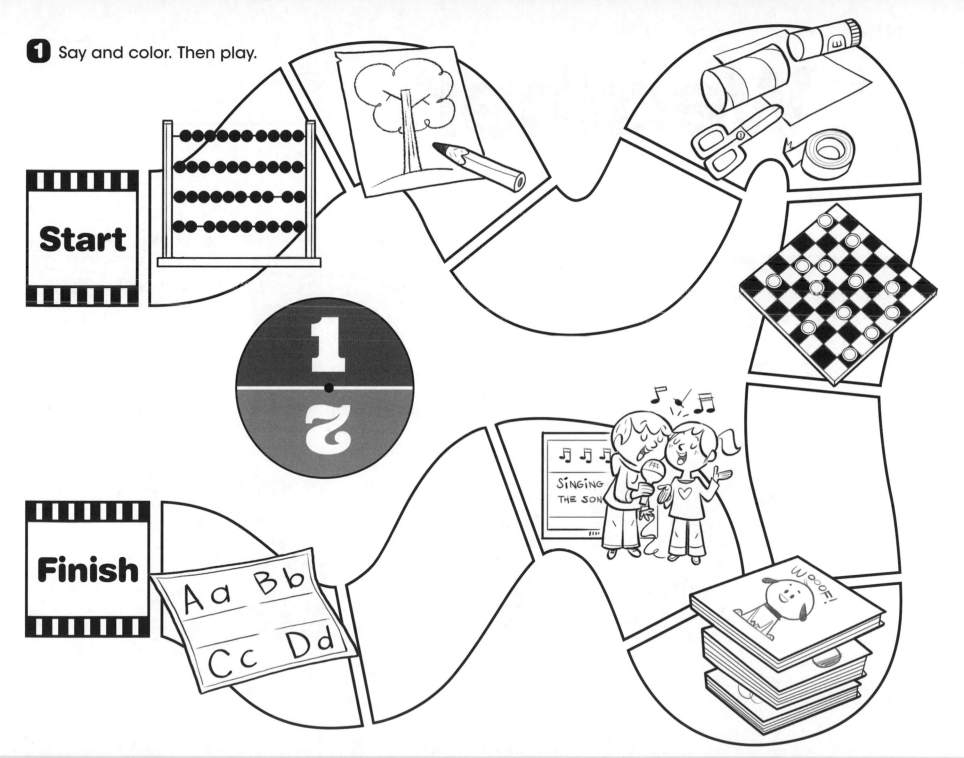

REVIEW: **NEW WORDS:** *count to ten, draw a picture, make a craft, play a game, read a book, sing a song, write letters*
STRUCTURE: *Let's draw a picture. OK, good idea!/No, thanks.*

9

2 Weather

1 TR: 2.1 Listen. Circle ✔ or ✗.

1 ✔ ✗

2 ✔ ✗

3 ✔ ✗

4 ✔ ✗

5 ✔ ✗

6 ✔ ✗

7 ✔ ✗

2 Point and say.

NEW WORDS: *cloudy, cold, hot, rainy, snowy, sunny, windy*

1 TR: 2.2 Listen and match. Then point and say.

1 2 3 4 5 6 7

STRUCTURE: *What's the weather like? It's sunny.*

1 TR: 2.3 Point and say. Then sing. Color.

2 Write ✔ or ✘.

VALUE   Be careful in the sun.

1 ☐

2 ☐

3 ☐

1 TR: 2.4 Listen and trace. Say.

1

man

2

van

2 Trace.

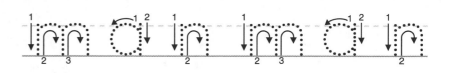

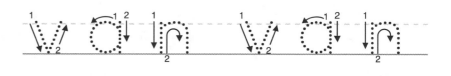

1 Color and say.

REVIEW: NEW WORDS: *cloudy, cold, hot, rainy, snowy, sunny, windy*
STRUCTURE: *What's the weather like? It's sunny.*

15

3 My Community

1 TR: **3.1** Listen and match.

1 2 3 4 5 6 7 8

2 Point and say.

NEW WORDS: *bus driver, dentist, doctor, firefighter, librarian, mail carrier, police officer, vet*

1 TR: 3.2 Listen and point. Then say.

STRUCTURE: *Is he/she a doctor? Yes, he/she is./No, he/she isn't.*

1 TR: **3.3** Listen and color.

2 Write ✔ or ✗.

VALUE Be polite.

1 ☐

2 ☐

3 ☐

1 TR: 3.4 Listen and trace. Say.

1

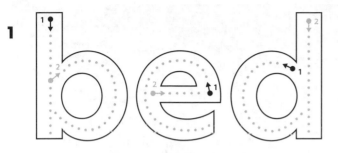

bed

2

red

2 Trace.

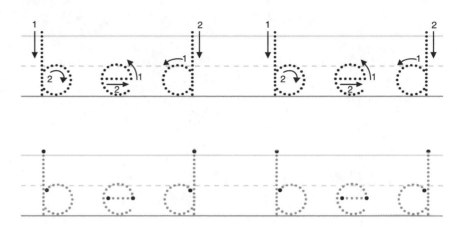

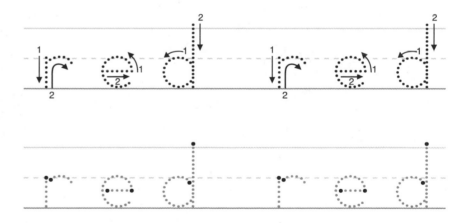

1 TR: 3.5 Listen and point. Then say.

VIDEO: SC: 6 *(optional)*   **Content Words:** *help, people*

1 TR: 3.6 Listen and match. Then say.

REVIEW: NEW WORDS: *bus driver, dentist, doctor, firefighter, librarian, mail carrier, police officer, vet*
STRUCTURE: *Is he/she a doctor? Yes, he/she is./No, he/she isn't.*

21

Make Some Noise!

1 TR: 4.1 Listen. Write ✔ or ✗.

1 ✓
2 ☐
3 ☐
4 ☐
5 ☐
6 ☐
7 ☐
8 ☐

2 Point and say.

NEW WORDS: *drums, guitar, piano, recorder, tambourine, trumpet, violin, xylophone*

1 TR: 4.2 Listen and match. Then point and say.

STRUCTURE: *He can play the piano. She can play the guitar.*

23

1 TR: 4.3 Listen and circle. Then sing and point.

2 Write ✔ or ✗.

VALUE   Work together.

1

2

3

2 Trace.

1

pet

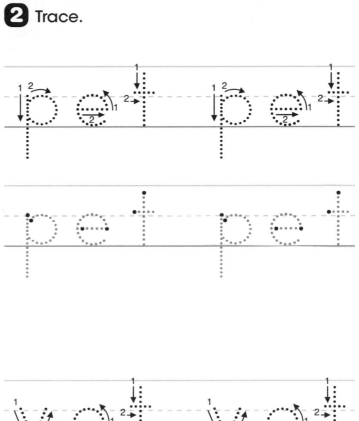

2

vet

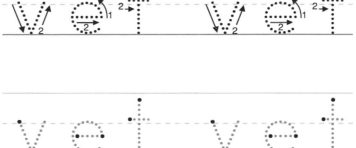

1 Point and say. Then color.

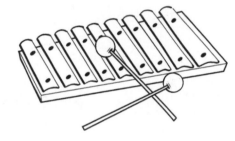

1 Say. Then play and do.

REVIEW: **NEW WORDS:** *drums, guitar, piano, recorder, tambourine, trumpet, violin, xylophone*
STRUCTURE: *He can play the piano. She can play the guitar.*

27

UNIT 5 Shapes Around Us

1 TR: 5.1 Listen and match.

1 2 3 4 5 6 7 8

2 Point and say.

NEW WORDS: *circle, diamond, hexagon, oval, rectangle, square, star, triangle*

STRUCTURE: *What are these? They're diamonds.*

1 TR: 5.3 Listen and color. Then sing.

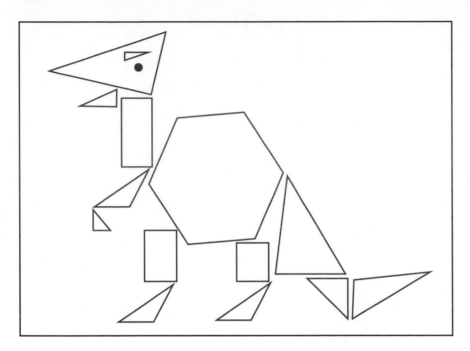

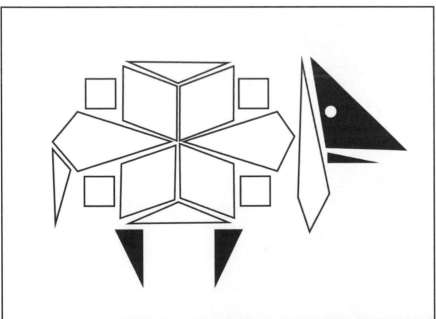

2 Write ✔ or ✗.

VALUE   Use your imagination.

1 ☐

2 ☐

3 ☐

1 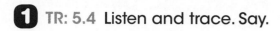 TR: 5.4 Listen and trace. Say.

1

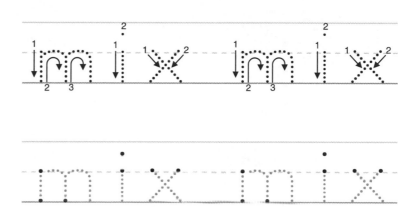

mix

2

six

2 Trace.

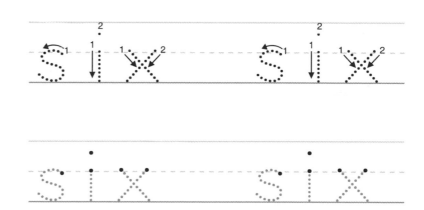

1 TR: 5.5 Listen and match. Then say.

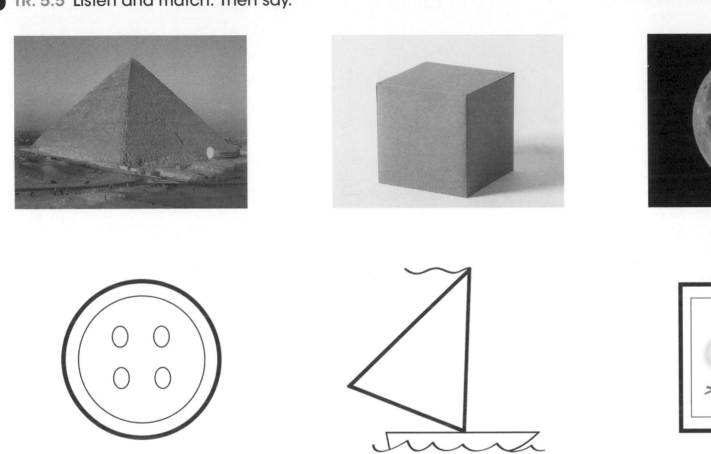

VIDEO: SC: 10 *(optional)* **Content Words:** *cube, flat, pyramid, sphere, world*

1 Say and color. Then play.

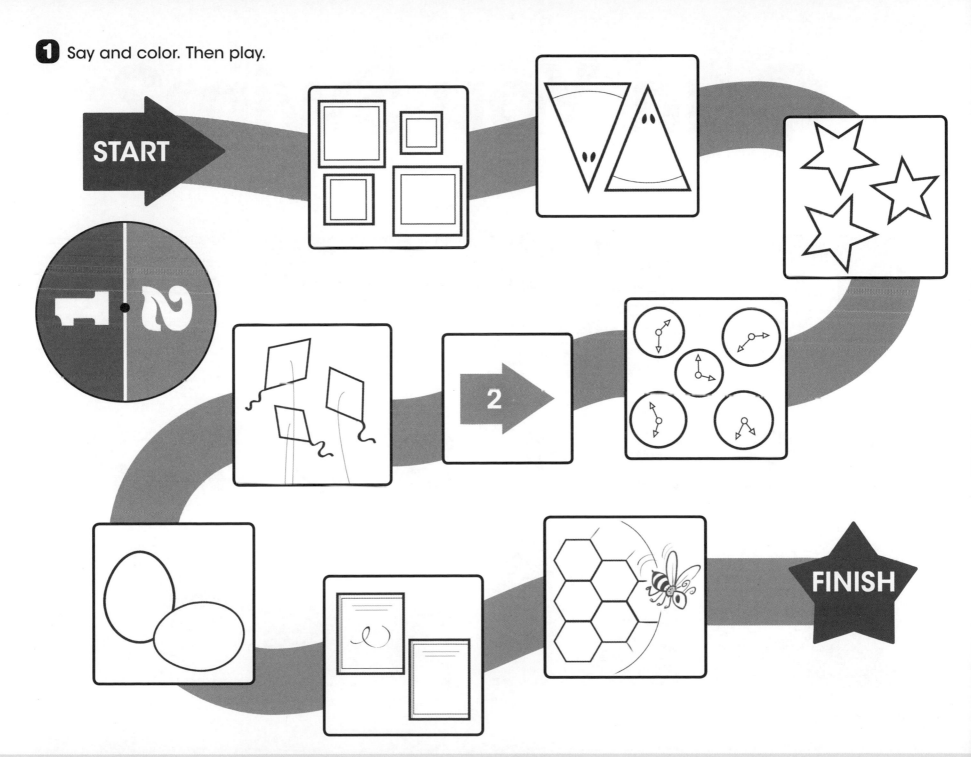

REVIEW: NEW WORDS: *circle, diamond, hexagon, oval, rectangle, square, star, triangle*
STRUCTURE: *What are these? They're diamonds.*

6 Can You Swim?

1 TR: 6.1 Listen and match.

1 2 3 4 5 6 7 8

2 Point and say.

NEW WORDS: *catch, climb, fly, kick, ride, skip, swim, throw*

1 TR: 6.2 Listen and circle. Then say.

STRUCTURE: *Can you skip? Yes, I can./No, I can't.*

35

1 **TR: 6.3** Listen and color.

2 Write ✔ or ✗.

VALUE Try again.

1 ☐

2 ☐

3 ☐

1 TR: 6.4 Listen and trace. Say.

2 Trace.

1

big

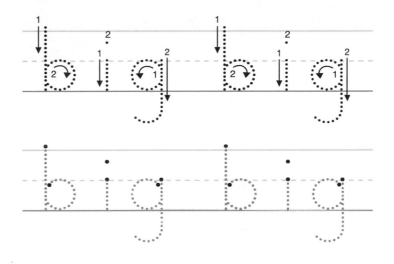

2

dig

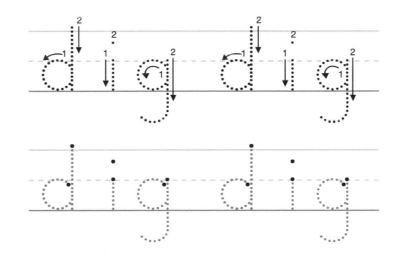

PHONICS: *big* and *dig*

1 TR: 6.5 Listen and match. Then say.

VIDEO: SC: 12 *(optional)* **Content Word:** *penguin*

1 Say and color. Then play.

REVIEW: NEW WORDS: *catch, climb, fly, kick, ride, skip, swim, throw*
STRUCTURE: *Can you skip? Yes, I can./No, I can't.*

39

1 TR: 7.1 Listen and circle ✔ or ✘.

1 ✔ ✘

2 ✔ ✘

3 ✔ ✘

4 ✔ ✘

5 ✔ ✘

6 ✔ ✘

7 ✔ ✘

8 ✔ ✘
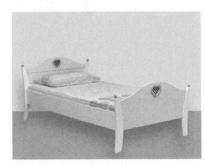

2 Point and say.

NEW WORDS: *bathroom, bedroom, kitchen, living room; bed, shelf, sink, sofa; welcome*

1 TR: 7.2 Listen and match.

1 2 3 4 5 6

STRUCTURE: *The picture is in the bathroom. The cars are under the bed.*

1 TR: 7.3 Listen and find. Then sing.

2 Write ✔ or ✘.

 VALUE Help at home.

1 ☐

2 ☐

3 ☐

1 Listen and trace. Say.

1

2 Trace.

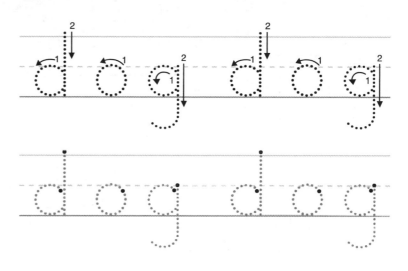

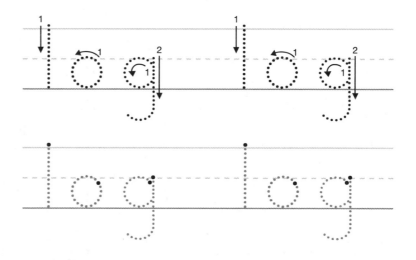

1 TR: 7.5 Listen and point.

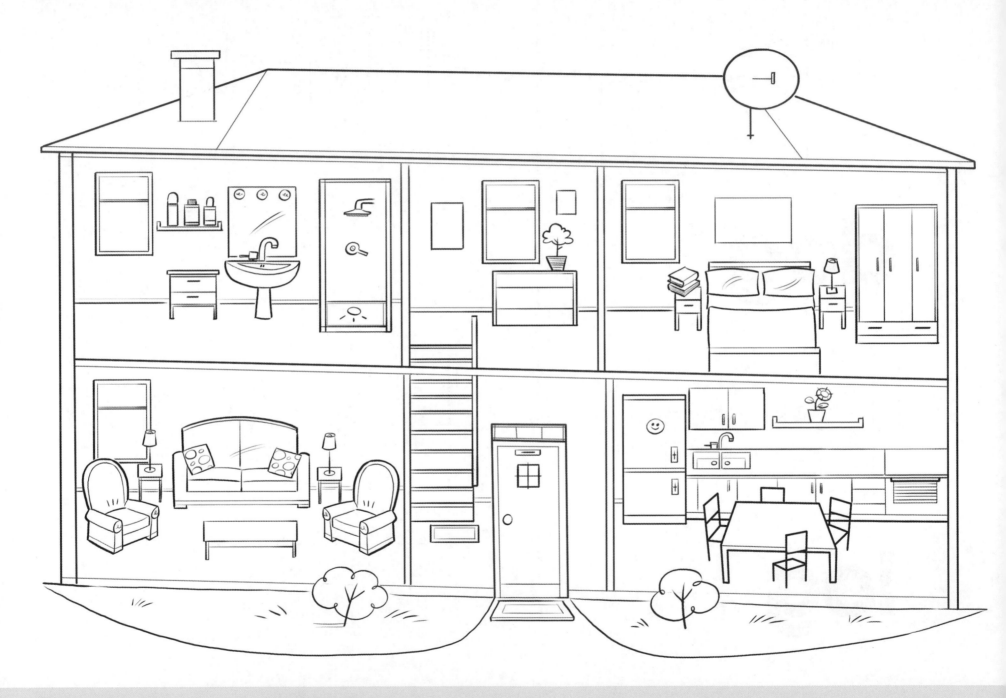

VIDEO: SC: 14 *(optional)*   **Content Words:** *apartment, city, country, garden, house*

1 Draw and say.

REVIEW: NEW WORDS: *bedroom, bathroom, kitchen, living room; bed, shelf, sink, sofa; welcome*
STRUCTURE: *The picture is in the bathroom. The cars are under the bed.*

45

1 TR: 8.1 Listen. Write ✔ or ✘.

1 ☐

2 ☐

3 ☐

4 ☐

5 ☐

6 ☐

7 ☐

8 ☐

2 Point and say.

1 What's different? Say.

1

2
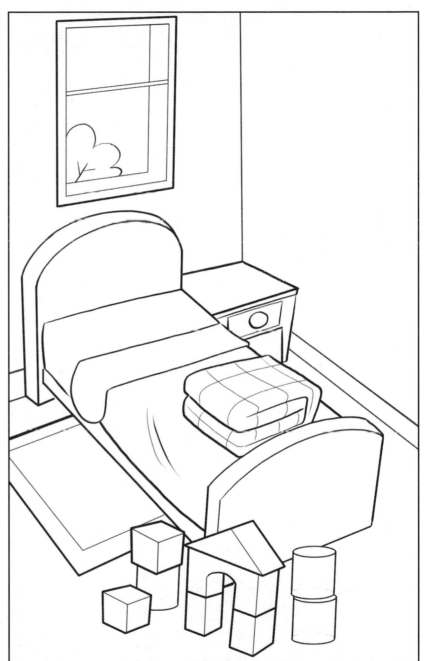

1 TR: 8.2 Listen and color.

2 Write ✔ or ✗.

VALUE   Be welcoming.

1 ☐

2 ☐

3 ☐

1

box

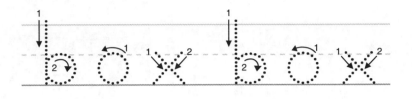

2

fox

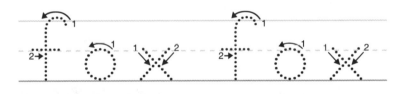

1

2

3

1 Color and say.

REVIEW: NEW WORDS: *blanket, door, lamp, pillow, rug, toy box, tree house, window*
STRUCTURE: *Is there a rug? Yes, there is./No, there isn't.*

51

UNIT 9 Under the Sea

1 TR: 9.1 Listen and match.

1 2 3 4 5 6 7 8

2 Point and say.

NEW WORDS: *crab, dolphin, jellyfish, octopus, seahorse, shark, starfish, turtle*

1 Play and say.

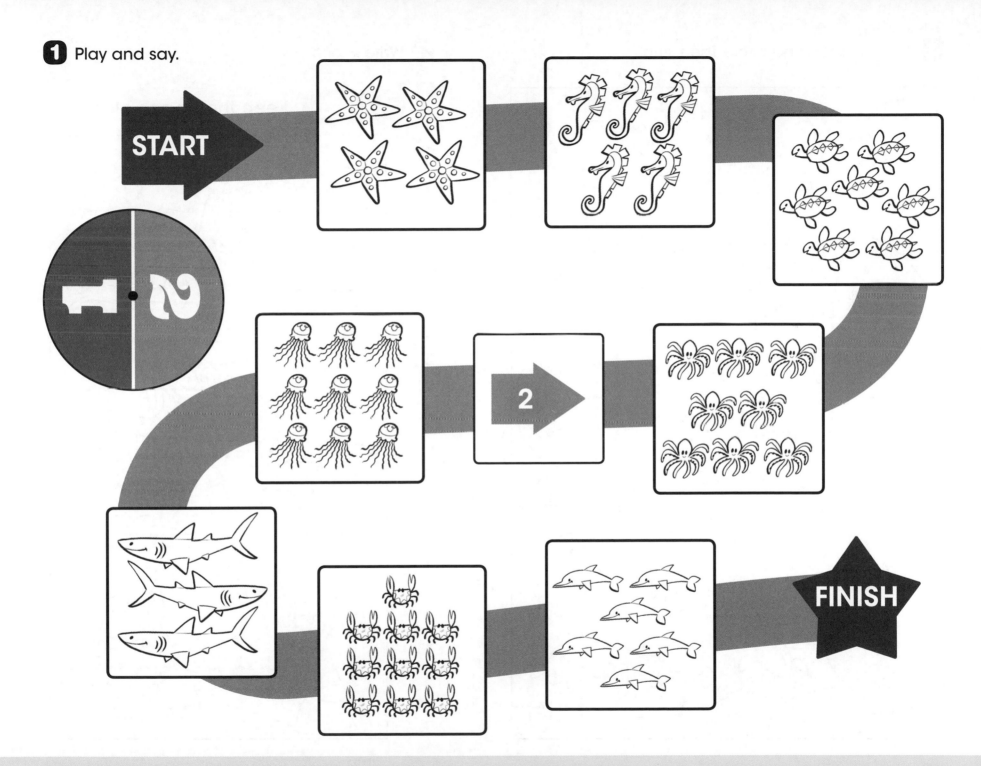

1 TR: 9.2 Listen and circle. Then sing.

2 Write ✔ or ✗.

VALUE   Keep the beach clean.

1 ☐

2 ☐

3 ☐

1 Listen and trace. Say.

2 Trace.

1

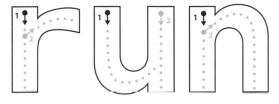

run

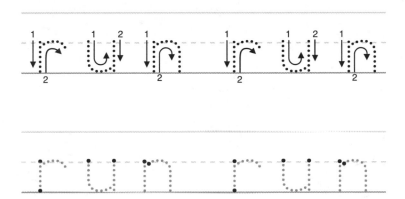

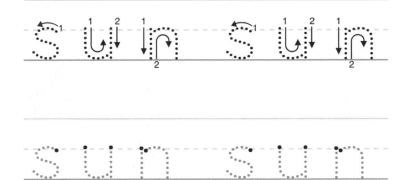

2

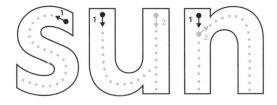

sun

1 TR: 9.4 Listen and point. Then color.

VIDEO: SC: 18 (optional)   Content Words: *beautiful, coral reef, eat*

1 Count and say. Then play.

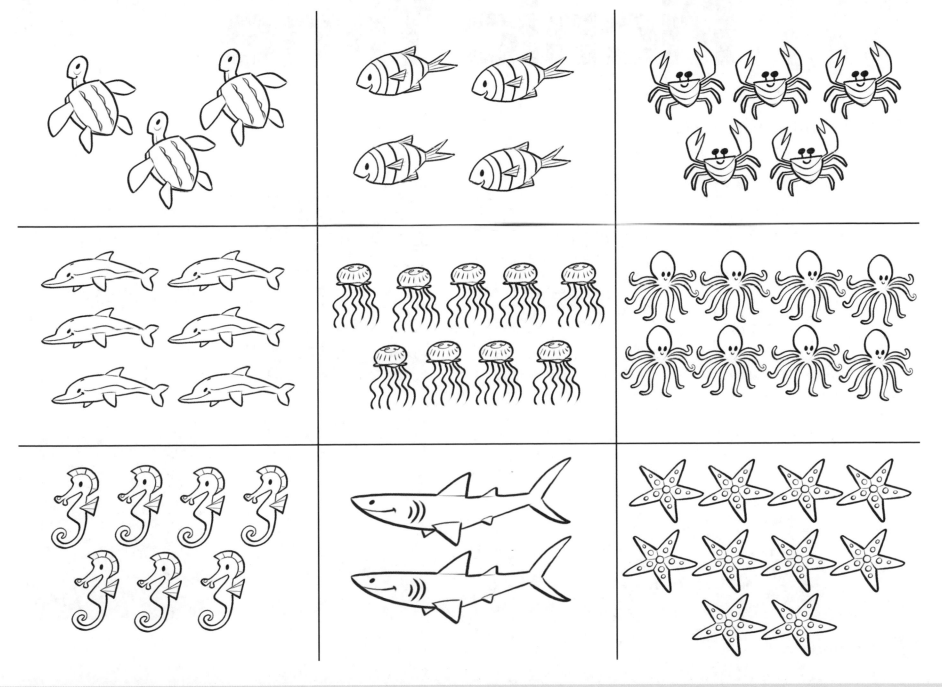

REVIEW: NEW WORDS: *crab, dolphin, jellyfish, octopus, seahorse, shark, starfish, turtle*
STRUCTURE: *How many crabs are there? There are fourteen crabs.*

57

1 TR: 10.1 Listen. Write ✔ or ✘.

1 ☐

2 ☐

3 ☐

4 ☐

5 ☐

6 ☐

7 ☐

8 ☐

2 Point and say.

1 TR: 10.2 Listen and circle. Then say.

1

2

3

4

5

6

STRUCTURE: *Do you like fruit? Yes, I do./No, I don't.*

1 TR: 10.3 Listen and color.

2 Write ✔ or ✗.

VALUE   Try new things.

1 ☐

2 ☐

3 ☐

1

bug

2

mug

2 Trace.

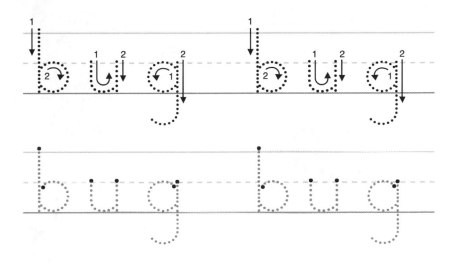

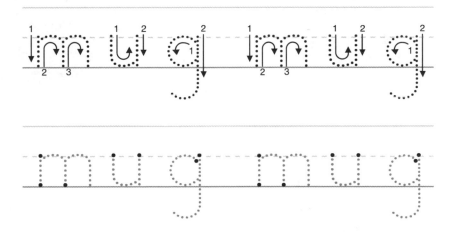

1 TR: 10.5 Match. Then listen and check.

1 Color. Draw and say.

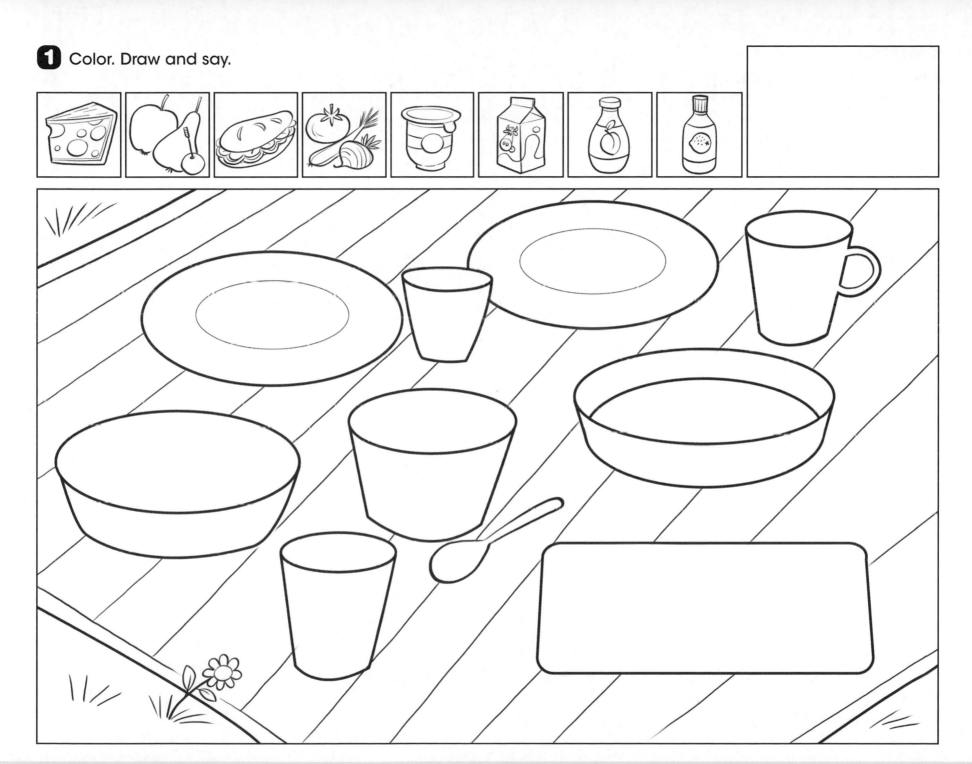

REVIEW: NEW WORDS: *cheese, fruit, juice, lemonade, picnic, sandwich, vegetables, yogurt*
STRUCTURE: *Do you like fruit? Yes, I do./No, I don't.*

63

CREDITS